3488000822929
BOOK CHARGING CARD

Accession No. _____ Call No. 976.1 PAR

Author _Parker, Janice_

Title _Alabama_

976.1
PAR

Parker, Janice
Alabama
3488 000082929

ALABAMA

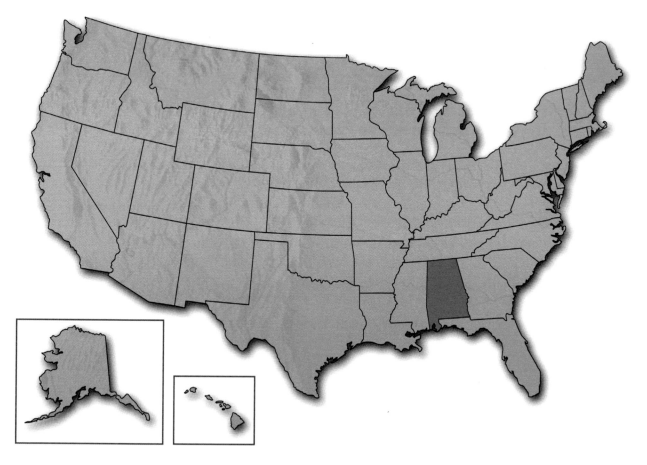

Janice Parker

Published by Weigl Publishers Inc.
123 South Broad Street, Box 227
Mankato, MN   56002
USA
Web site: http://www.weigl.com

Library of Congress Cataloging-in-Publication Data

Parker, Janice.
   Alabama / Janice Parker.
       p. cm. -- (A kid's guide to American states)
   Includes bibliographical references (p.) and index.
   ISBN 1-930954-23-9 (lib. bdg.)
      1. Alabama--Juvenile literature. [1. Alabama.] I. Title. II. Series.

F326.3 .P37 2001
976.1--dc21

2001026141

ISBN 1-930954-66-2 (pbk.)

Printed in the United States of America
1 2 3 4 5 6 7 8 9 10   05 04 03 02 01

Project Coordinator
Michael Lowry
Substantive Editor
Rennay Craats
Copy Editor
Bryan Pezzi
Designers
Warren Clark
Terry Paulhus
Photo Researcher
Diana Marshall

Photograph Credits

Every reasonable effort has been made to trace ownership and to obtain permission to reprint copyright material. The publishers would be pleased to have any errors or omissions brought to their attention so that they may be corrected in subsequent printings.

CONTENTS

Alabama's beautiful Mobile-Tensaw Delta is home to sixty-seven endangered species.

INTRODUCTION

Alabama is a state of fascinating places and friendly people. The landscape offers a beautiful mix of expansive forests, sandy coastal plains, and bountiful farmlands.

The land has always played an important role in Alabama's economy. The state once depended primarily upon the cotton industry, but over the years agriculture has expanded into other areas. Today, Alabama produces a wide variety of crops, such as soybeans, peanuts, and melons.

Industry plays an important role as well. Alabama's abundance of natural resources provides the state with many economic opportunities. The ground yields valuable minerals, while the rivers provide important transportation routes and can be harnessed to produce **hydroelectricity.**

QUICK FACTS

Alabama's official nickname is "The Yellowhammer State." The nickname comes from the uniforms worn by Alabama soldiers during the American Civil War. The uniforms had yellow trimmings that resembled the yellow patches on the wings of the yellowhammer bird.

Other Alabama nicknames include "The Heart of Dixie," "The Cotton State," "The Cotton Plantation State," and "The Camellia State."

Alabama's motto is "We Dare Defend Our Rights."

The Jasmine Hill southern garden was created in the 1920s as a tribute to classical Greek art and culture. Over thirty Greek statues and fountains can be found in the garden.

The Birmingham International Airport employs more than 4,000 people and services about 3 million passengers each year.

Getting There

Alabama is located in the southeastern United States, also known as the Deep South. It is bordered by Tennessee to the north, Georgia to the east, Florida and the Gulf Coast to the south, and Mississippi to the west.

The Birmingham International Airport is the busiest in the state. Other large airports can be found in Huntsville, Mobile, and Montgomery. Amtrak offers train travel through several Alabama cities, while Greyhound provides bus service across the state. Three interstate highways pass through Birmingham—the I-20, the I-59, and the I-65. The I-10 runs through Mobile. More than 94,000 miles of highway cover the state.

QUICK FACTS

Alabama's state flag was adopted in 1895. It consists of a crimson St. Andrew's cross on a white background.

The flag of the Confederate States of America was designed and first flown in Alabama in 1861.

The city of Mobile, on the Gulf Coast, is one of the most important **seaports** in the United States. Mobile is located on the Intracoastal Waterway, which is used to ship goods along the United States.

When Birmingham's airport opened in 1931, it took nineteen hours to fly from Birmingham to Los Angeles.

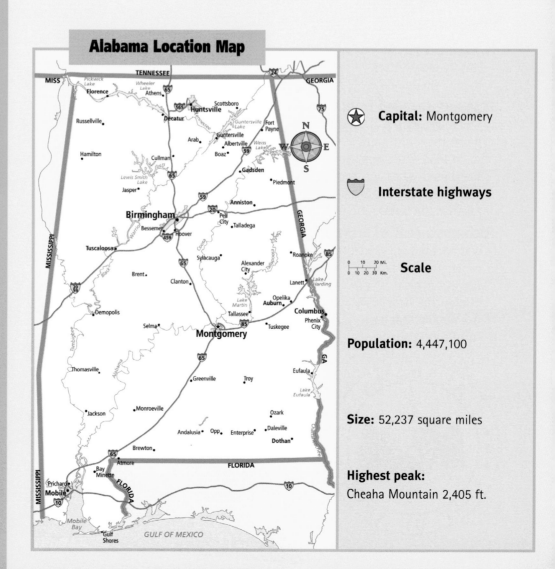

Alabama Location Map

Capital: Montgomery

Interstate highways

Scale

Population: 4,447,100

Size: 52,237 square miles

Highest peak: Cheaha Mountain 2,405 ft.

During the American Civil War, Alabama left the United States of America and took up arms with the Confederate States of America.

Throughout its history, Alabama has been the site of many conflicts. In the state's early years, Europeans and Native Americans fought for control of the region. Later on, European countries clashed with each other in their attempt to gain ownership over Alabama. Five countries have ruled over the state—Spain, France, Great Britain, the Confederate States, and the United States.

Early nineteenth century Alabama was divided over the issue of slavery. Slavery was the successful backbone of the state's thriving cotton industry. In 1861, Alabama voted to **secede** from the Union, rather than abolish slavery. During the American Civil War, Alabama played a crucial role in the development of the Confederate States of America. Montgomery, known as "The Cradle of the Confederacy," hosted the first meeting of the seceding states and became the first capital of the Confederacy.

The First White House of the Confederacy was located in Montgomery. It served as the home of Confederate President Jefferson Davis from February 4, 1861 to May 21, 1861. The Confederate capital was later moved to Richmond in Virginia.

Rosa Parks's refusal to give up her seat on a segregated bus resulted in the Montgomery boycott.

In the twentieth century, the civil rights movement in Alabama gained strength as African Americans struggled for freedom and equality. In 1955, Rosa Parks refused to give up her seat on a bus. At the time, it was required by law that African Americans give up their seats to people of European heritage. Her arrest caused the Montgomery **boycott**, led by a young minister, Martin Luther King, Jr. For 382 days, African Americans and others refused to use the city transit system in protest.

The Montgomery boycott resulted in the United States Supreme Court decision that bus **segregation** was **unconstitutional**. It also established Martin Luther King, Jr. as a national hero and defender of civil rights. Today, **desegregation** and the election of African Americans to public office are helping to improve race relations in Alabama.

QUICK FACTS

The 16th Street Baptist Church was the location of a bombing that killed four African-American girls on September 16, 1963. The bomb was planted by members of the terrorist group the Ku Klux Klan.

Martin Luther King, Jr. was minister of the Dexter Avenue Baptist Church in Montgomery. The church served as a meeting place for participants in the Montgomery boycott.

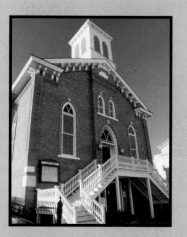

In 1965, Martin Luther King, Jr. led a march from Selma to Montgomery. The Freedom March was a protest against the many voting restrictions placed upon African Americans.

The Sipsey Wilderness area is the most popular backpacking destination in Alabama.

LAND AND CLIMATE

Alabama is made up of five natural regions. Three of these regions—the Appalachian Plateau, the Piedmont Plateau, and the Ridge and Valley region—make up the Appalachian Highlands. The Appalachian Plateau includes the southern part of the Appalachian Mountain range.

The Interior Low Plateau, in the northwestern corner of the state, has excellent farmland. The Gulf Coastal Plain is the largest region in Alabama and contains an area called the Black Belt. Named for its fertile soil, the Black Belt is also known for its agriculture. The area is also a source of lumber.

Alabama has long, warm summers and short, mild winters. In summer, temperatures are in the mid-80's Fahrenheit, while winter temperatures range from 44°F to 57°F. Thundershowers are common, and the state receives a considerable amount of rain.

The Kymulga Grist Mill Park is home to one of Alabama's oldest water-powered grist mills.

NATURAL RESOURCES

There are more than 663,000 acres of national forest in Alabama.

Alabama has a wide variety of natural resources. Forests cover more than two-thirds of the state. Fertile soils, a long growing season, and abundant rainfall are key to the state's agriculture. Alabama is rich in coal, limestone, **bauxite**, and white marble. The abundance of iron ore, or hematite, has contributed to the strong iron and steel industries in the state. Natural gas is one of the most valuable resources in Alabama. It accounts for more than one-half of the state's income from **fossil fuels**.

Alabama's rivers provide water for **irrigation** and recreation. Hydroelectricity is generated at several dams, including Muscle Shoals. Alabama's beautiful landscape is another valuable resource. Trees, flowers, caves, and wildlife preserves help to bring billions of tourist dollars into the state each year.

QUICK FACTS

Hematite, a primary source of iron, is the official state mineral of Alabama.

Alabama has nearly 22 million acres of forest, which contain more than 15 billion trees. More than 150 million trees are planted each year in the state.

Alabama produces some of the world's finest white marble.

Alabama has 53 miles of coastline.

Alabama's coastal waters are a bountiful resource for the state's fishing industry.

The Cahaba River is one of the few rivers in Alabama which is not heavily dammed. As a result, it supports a large variety of plant and animal life.

PLANTS AND ANIMALS

The beautiful, pinkshell azalea can be found throughout Alabama.

More than 125 species of trees can be found in Alabama. Pine and oak trees grow throughout the state. Black walnut and sweet gum trees are plentiful. Spanish moss grows on many of the state's trees. Alabama has many flowering trees and shrubs, including magnolia, azalea, dogwood, and rhododendron. Common wildflowers, such as thistle, trillium, and prairie clover, add a splash of color to the landscape. Mistletoe, blackberries, huckleberries, and mountain laurels all grow throughout the state.

In 1992, Alabama created the Forever Wild Program, which is devoted to protecting the state's wildlife. Funding comes from interest on the sale of natural gas. The program also preserves land for outdoor recreation and research.

Paddlefish are just one of the many animals that are protected by Alabama's Forever Wild Program.

While there is a large number of bobcats in Alabama, they are rarely spotted in the wild.

Alabama's forests are filled with a variety of animals, including bobcats, red and gray foxes, raccoons, squirrels, weasels, otters, and opossums. Larger mammals are not as numerous, although there are black bears in the south and white-tailed deer in the west. Bird-watchers keep their eyes open for the state's many species of birds, including bald eagles, ospreys, brown pelicans, bluebirds, and great blue herons.

Bass, trout, and catfish can be found in Alabama's lakes and rivers. Mullets, red snappers, crabs, oysters, and shrimps live in the waters off the Gulf Coast. Alligators are found in swamps in the southern region of the state. About 35,000 alligators inhabit the Mobile Delta area. Many poisonous snakes make their home in Alabama. These include the rattlesnake, the coral snake, and the water moccasin.

The Jaycee Rattlesnake Rodeo attracts thousands of people to Opp, Alabama. The rodeo features rattlesnake races and snake displays. Some of the featured snakes can weigh up to 11 pounds.

QUICK FACTS

Alabama has a state saltwater fish, the fighting tarpon, and a state freshwater fish, the largemouth bass.

Largemouth Bass

There have been only five recorded alligator attacks on people in Alabama. No one has ever died from an alligator attack in the state.

Alabama is home to a very rare animal, the dismalite. Dismalites are worms that glow in the dark.

The great Onyx Cathedral, in the DeSoto Caverns, is larger than a football field and higher than a twelve-story building.

TOURISM

Tourism has created over 122,000 jobs in Alabama. Tourists spend approximately $5.4 billion in the state each year. Visitors come to Alabama to enjoy the warm southern climate. Fishing, boating, and other water activities are popular in the state's many lakes, rivers, and reservoirs. The Gulf of Mexico is an ideal place for ocean fishing.

The many caves and caverns in the northeastern part of Alabama are also popular with tourists. The state has more than 3,000 known caves, making it an ideal spot for **spelunking**. The 14-acre Cathedral Caverns is known for having the world's largest **stalagmite** forest.

The United States Space and Rocket Center, in Huntsville, is the world's largest space travel attraction. The center has more than 1,500 space artifacts on display, and is home to one of NASA's Space Camps for children. For five days, children can live like astronauts, experience weightlessness in the Gravity Trainer, eat freeze-dried food, and operate futuristic jet packs.

The United States Space and Rocket Center is home to the largest collection of rockets and space memorabilia in the world.

QUICK FACTS

The well-known Looking Glass Lakes, in the Sequoyah Caverns, are crystal clear pools that reflect the ceiling of the caverns. This effect tricks visitors into thinking that they are looking into a deep gorge rather than a shallow pool of water.

A skeleton of a prehistoric man was found in a cave at the Russell Cave National Monument.

A popular tourist attraction in Mobile is the USS *Alabama*. The ship is anchored in Mobile Bay and is open to the public.

The Sloss Furnaces were built in 1881 in Birmingham. The two giant furnaces produced iron for nearly 90 years.

QUICK FACTS

Alabama is ranked second in the nation in the production of catfish. The catfish are often raised on farms. Farmers flood their croplands to create artificial ponds.

Alabama is the only state that contains all of the natural resources needed to make iron and steel.

Alabama is the largest supplier of cast-iron and steel-pipe products in the United States.

The Sloss Furnaces in Birmingham were designated a National Historic Site in 1983. The furnaces once employed nearly 500 workers and produced 400 tons of pig iron per day.

INDUSTRY

Fishing is a $50 million industry in Alabama. The state has both freshwater and saltwater commercial fishing. Shrimps are the most valuable saltwater seafood. Oysters, blue crabs, and red snappers are also important. Buffalofish, mussels, and catfish are caught in freshwater streams.

Alabama's abundance of mineral resources means that mining is very important to the state's economy. The underground coal mines in western Alabama are some of the deepest in the nation.

The production of iron and steel, in the Birmingham area, is one of the main industries in Alabama. Steel production occurs primarily in Birmingham, Decatur, and Gadsden. **Fabricated metals**, such as cast-iron pipes and metal valves, are also produced in the area.

Bayou La Batre is known as the "Seafood Capital of Alabama." This small fishing village is located in the southwestern corner of the state.

Cotton is still a leading industry in Alabama, but mechanical pickers now harvest most of the crops.

GOODS AND SERVICES

Cotton was once Alabama's most important product. The invasion of the **boll weevil** in 1915 destroyed a large proportion of the state's cotton plants, forcing farmers to diversify their crops. Instead of planting only cotton, they began to plant other crops as well. Corn and soybeans are planted in the southern part of Alabama. Peanuts, pecans, hay, oats, tobacco, and wheat are other important crops. The state also produces many fruits and vegetables, including peaches, apples, watermelons, beans, potatoes, and sweet potatoes.

Huntsville is known for its production of missiles. It was workers in Alabama that built the first rocket to put humans on the moon. The Marshall Space Flight Center, in Huntsville, is where NASA conducts rocket tests and trains astronauts.

The Neutral Buoyancy Simulator at the Marshall Space Flight Center allows astronauts to practice working without gravity.

The pulp and paper industry is another valuable source of income for Alabama. It includes the producers of sanitary paper products, box manufacturers, and pulp and paper mills. Chemical manufacturers in Alabama produce paint, fertilizer, and varnish. **Textile** mills, lumber mills, meat-packing plants, and industrial-machinery plants are also important.

Alabama's waterways help the state transport goods. Ships bring goods to the state and unload them at the Alabama State Docks in Mobile Bay. The Alabama State Docks operates a system of 376 inland docks, 37 cargo berths, and about 4 million square feet of storage space. The ships export coal, iron, steel, petroleum products, pulp and other wood products, soybeans, and wheat.

The Alabama State Docks employs more than 370 workers and covers nearly 3,500 acres of coastline.

The Mercedez-Benz automobile plant in Tuscaloosa contributes about $1.3 billion per year to Alabama's economy. The visitor center offers a glimpse of the company's history.

QUICK FACTS

Wholesale and retail trade is the leading service industry in Alabama. Major retail businesses include automobile dealerships and food stores.

Alabama's bee colonies produce more than 1 million pounds of honey each year.

Bruno's, a large chain of grocery stores in the South, is based out of Birmingham.

Alabama had the first state-owned educational television system in the nation.

The public school system is one of Alabama's major employers.

Computer electronics and other high-technology industries are located in and around Huntsville.

FIRST NATIONS

The Creek houses of the late-1700s combined horizontal logs with mud. The mud acted as insulation.

Mobile is named after the Maubilian people, who lived in the area during the early part of the eighteenth century.

Chief Sequoyah, the son of a Cherokee mother and a British father, created a written alphabet for the Cherokee language in 1821. As a result, the Cherokee were able to publish their own books and newspapers.

The mounds built by Alabama's early inhabitants were as high as 60 feet.

Archeological sites contain evidence of people living in Alabama as long as 10,000 years ago. These early peoples were hunters who used caves for shelter. By about 1,000 BC, they began to plant crops and build permanent settlements. Later, they lived in villages built around large mounds of earth. The mounds were an important part of their culture. These early inhabitants are sometimes called the Mound Builders.

Soon after, other groups of Native Peoples began to settle the Alabama area. By the eighteenth century, Native Americans in the region had organized into four major nations—the Cherokee, the Creek, the Choctaw, and the Chickasaw. By the 1830s, the United States government had forced these groups to move from their homes in Alabama to reservations in Oklahoma, to make room for European settlement.

The Choctaw Fancy Dancers, at Moundville's Native American Festival, re-create traditional ceremonies with their dances of dazzling, moving colors and swirling feathers.

Hernando de Soto was a Spanish explorer during the 1500s.

QUICK FACTS

Hernando de Soto's group introduced many European diseases to the Native Peoples in Alabama. Without **immunity** to the new diseases, thousands of Native Americans became sick and many died.

In 1689, French explorers claimed all of the land that was drained by the Mississippi River for France. The area was called the Louisiana Territory.

EXPLORERS AND MISSIONARIES

The first Europeans to reach the Alabama area were Spanish explorers. This group included Alonso Alvarez de Piñeda, who sailed into Mobile Bay in 1519. Around 1540, Spaniard Hernando de Soto and his army moved up from the Gulf of Mexico in search of gold. He raided Native-American villages, took hostages, and tortured Native Peoples for information and for food. De Soto's treatment of Native Americans resulted in many conflicts. One of the worst of these battles was with Chief Tuscaloosa at Maubila. The battle resulted in the deaths of several thousand Native Americans and left de Soto's troops severely weakened.

In 1559, Don Tristan de Luna traveled from Mexico to Mobile, with 500 soldiers and 1,000 colonists, to start a settlement. They also looked unsuccessfully for gold. In 1561, a fierce storm destroyed much of their food and supplies, forcing them to return to Mexico.

Hernando de Soto's army clashed with Chief Tuscaloosa and his forces at Maubila. Tuscaloosa was retaliating against de Soto's terrible treatment of Native Americans.

EARLY SETTLERS

In 1702, French-Canadian explorer Jean-Baptiste Le Moyne, Sieur de Bienville, established a French settlement on the Mobile River. It was a trading post called Fort Louis. After a flood washed the post away in 1711, it was renamed Fort Condé de la Mobile and was moved to the site of present-day Mobile. The fort was the center of the French government for the Louisiana colony during the early 1700s.

Soon, settlers began to arrive from France and Canada. Early French settlers nearly starved to death waiting for supply ships to arrive from France. In 1719, the French brought slaves over from Africa. The slaves cleared fields and harvested crops. Alabama's cotton industry relied heavily on the labor of African slaves.

The star design of Fort Condé allowed soldiers within the fort to have an all-around view for defense.

QUICK FACTS

When the British took over Fort Condé, they renamed it Fort Charlotte.

General Andrew Jackson led many successful battles against the Creek Confederacy during the War of 1812.

General Andrew Jackson supervised the construction of Fort Jackson on the ruins of the old French Fort Toulouse.

Dr. George Washington Carver's innovations in the agricultural sciences led southern farmers to plant new types of crops other than cotton.

France gave up its North American colonies at the end of the French and Indian War in 1763. These colonies, which included the Alabama region, fell under the control of Great Britain. When the American Revolution ended in 1783, northern Alabama became part of the United States, while Mobile and southern Alabama were ruled by Spain. The United States seized Mobile from the Spanish in the War of 1812, and in 1817, Alabama became a territory of the United States.

Settlers soon moved into the Alabama territory to take advantage of its fertile land. By 1819, enough people lived in the territory to qualify it for statehood. Alabama joined the Union on December 14, 1819. During the next ten years, the state's population more than doubled, as settlers poured in from Tennessee, South Carolina, and North Carolina. The population grew from 127,900 people in 1820 to 309,530 people in 1830. Cotton plantations, which depended on slave labor for their profits, sprung up across the state.

Fort Gaines, on Dauphin Island, served as a Confederate fort during the American Civil War. The fort surrendered to Union forces at the Battle of Mobile Bay in 1864.

The Salute to Germany, at the Birmingham International Festival, is a celebration of German culture and heritage.

POPULATION

About 4.4 million people live in Alabama. Around two-thirds of Alabamians live in cities, towns, or villages with populations of more than 2,500 people. The largest cities are Birmingham, Mobile, Montgomery, Huntsville, and Tuscaloosa. Alabama has a **population density** of nearly 86 people per square mile. This is greater than the national average, which is 77 people per square mile.

Alabamians of European heritage make up the largest percentage of the population at 74 percent. African Americans are second at 25 percent. Asians and Native Americans together account for less than 1 percent.

Around three-quarters of people over the age of 25 are high-school graduates, while one-fifth have college degrees.

QUICK FACTS

Alabama is made up of sixty-seven counties.

Many important civil rights activists were born in Alabama, including Rosa Parks, Ralph Abernathy, and Coretta Scott King.

More than twenty-five languages are spoken in Alabama, but most people in the state speak English as their first or only language.

Birmingham is known as the "Pittsburgh of the South." The city is home to a large number of steel mills, factories, and skyscrapers.

Richard Arrington became the first African-American mayor of Birmingham in 1979.

Each year, in May, thousands of Alabamians attend the World-Class Music Festival in downtown Birmingham.

The State Capitol, in Montgomery, was designated a National Historic Site in 1960.

Alabama is represented in the United States government by two senators and seven members of the House of Representatives. The state has nine presidential electoral votes.

On Sunday March 7, 1965, about 600 protesters began a march from Selma to Montgomery. They were stopped violently by the police at the Edmund Pettus Bridge. The day has become known as "Bloody Sunday."

POLITICS AND GOVERNMENT

Alabama is governed under its sixth constitution, which was adopted in 1901. The Alabama government is divided into three branches—the executive, the legislative, and the judicial. The governor, who is elected for a four-year term, is the head of the executive branch. The governor's main purpose is to make sure that state laws are enforced. The secretary of state, the state treasurer, and the attorney general are part of the executive branch of government.

The legislative branch is responsible for creating laws. It is made up of a House of Representatives and a Senate. Alabama has 105 representatives and 37 senators, all elected for four-year terms.

The judicial branch includes the Supreme Court, the court of civil appeals, and the court of criminal appeals. All judges and justices are elected for six-year terms.

The National Voting Rights Museum and Institute, in Selma, honors those who have advanced the struggle for African-American voting rights. Jesse Jackson is among the inductees to the museum's Hall of Fame.

CULTURAL GROUPS

The Freedom March was organized to protest the restrictions placed upon African-American voters.

Martin Luther King, Jr.

Alabama's rich culture has a strong connection to the civil rights movement. The Birmingham Civil Rights District serves as an important reminder of the African-American struggle for human rights. The district occupies six city blocks and includes the Birmingham Civil Rights Institute, the Kelly Ingram Park, the Carver Theater, and the 16th Street Baptist Church.

Birmingham's Fourth Avenue Business District is a major African-American cultural area, such as Harlem in New York or Bronzeville in Chicago. It was once home to more than 3,400 African-American businesses, some of which still operate today. In the early 1900s, the district was the only place that African-American businesses were permitted to operate. The area thrived with restaurants, financial companies, barbershops, theaters, and nightclubs. Today, many of the buildings have been renovated and become part of the historic Civil Rights District.

The Alabama Jazz Hall of Fame is located at the old Carver Theater. The theater was part of Birmingham's Fourth Avenue Business District.

The Birmingham Civil Rights Institute displays a replica of a bus ridden by the Freedom Riders.

The Birmingham Civil Rights Institute was created in 1992 to educate people about African-American culture and the fight for equality. Exhibits show what it was like for African Americans to live in a segregated society—from using separate drinking fountains and classrooms to attending civil rights rallies. The institute serves as a reminder of the African-American struggle in the United States.

Alabama's European culture is celebrated in the city of Mobile. The Mobile **Mardi Gras** is a combination of both French and Spanish traditions. Dozens of groups build elegant floats and parade through downtown Mobile. Mobile's first Mardi Gras parade consisted of one decorated coal wagon hitched up to a mule. Today, there are about twenty separate parades held over several weeks.

QUICK FACTS

In 1964, President John F. Kennedy ordered the National Guard to help usher African-American students into the University of Alabama. Prior to this, the university had not allowed African Americans to attend.

The number of African-American students attending integrated schools in Alabama jumped from 15 percent to 80 percent between 1969 and 1970.

In 1704, Mobile became the first city in the country to hold a Mardi Gras celebration. This happened sixty-two years before New Orleans began its celebrations.

Participants in Mobile's Mardi Gras parades wear masks and throw candies, beads, and other gifts to the crowds.

The Alabama Jazz Hall of Fame honors great jazz musicians who have ties to the state, such as Nat King Cole and Duke Ellington.

ARTS AND ENTERTAINMENT

Many important writers have come from Alabama. Booker T. Washington, the son of a slave, became a well-known educator. He wrote many books, including his **autobiographical** *Up from Slavery*. Washington started the Tuskegee Normal and Industrial Institute, a school for rural African-American youths, which later became Tuskegee University. Helen Keller was an acclaimed author and lecturer from Tuscumbia. Keller, who was blind and deaf, became an inspiration to many by learning to speak and read braille despite her disabilities. Birmingham's Fannie Flagg wrote *Fried Green Tomatoes at the Whistle Stop Café*. The novel was made into a film starring Jessica Tandy and Kathy Bates. Alabamian Harper Lee won a Pulitzer Prize for her 1960 novel, *To Kill a Mockingbird*. Since its publication, *To Kill a Mockingbird* has never been out of print, and is one of the most widely read books in the English language.

Truman Capote grew up in Monroeville. He became known for such books as *Breakfast at Tiffany's* and *In Cold Blood*. Harper Lee based the character of Dill in *To Kill a Mockingbird* on Capote. *Breakfast at Tiffany's* was made into a successful movie starring Audrey Hepburn.

Before becoming well known as a singer, Alabama's Nat King Cole was a jazz pianist.

The Tuskegee University pays tribute to Booker T. Washington with a statue that depicts him helping an African-American slave out of the shadow of slavery and into the light of education.

In celebration of the state's talented musicians, the Alabama Music Hall of Fame was built in 1987.

Traditional music is played throughout Alabama. Jazz, blues, gospel, country, and rock musicians from Alabama are internationally renowned. Many Alabama musicians have been inducted into the Alabama Music Hall of Fame, and given the Lifework Award for Performing Achievement. The 12,500-square-foot Hall of Fame showcases music from the past and the present. Nat King Cole, Dinah Washington, Tammy Wynette, Wilson Pickett, and The Temptations are just a few Alabama recording artists who have achieved recognition from the hall.

Hank Williams, sometimes called the "father of modern country music," was born in 1923 in Georgiana. At a time when most other country-music singers performed other people's songs, Hank was unique in that he wrote his own music and created his own sound. During his lifetime, Hank had eleven number-one songs on the music charts. He was inducted into the Country Music Hall of Fame in 1961.

QUICK FACTS

Alabama's official state song is "Alabama."

An album of duets sung by Hank Williams and his son, Hank Williams Jr., won a Grammy Award in 1989 for Best Country Vocal Collaboration. The voice of the senior Hank came from remastered tapes of his old music.

Singer Tammy Wynette, known as the "first lady of country," was from Red Bay. Her song "Stand By Your Man" was the best-selling single in country music for fifteen years. She was the first female country artist to sell 1 million records.

Hank Williams was inducted into the Alabama Music Hall of Fame in 1985, winning the Lifework Award for Performing Achievement.

The Robert Trent Jones Golf Trail is the longest golf course ever created.

SPORTS

Alabama is a proud supporter of sports. The state has a history of producing world-class athletes. University football teams are very popular. Many of the state's teams, such as the University of Alabama's Crimson Tide and Auburn University's Auburn Tigers, share intense rivalries. Many National Football League players, including Burt Starr, Kevin Green, and Ken Stabler, are from Alabama.

Avid golfers travel to Alabama to play the 378-hole Robert Trent Jones Golf Trail. The trail includes twenty-one golf courses at eight different locations across the state. Outdoor recreation can also be found in Alabama's twenty-four state parks. The parks offer activities for children and adults, such as swimming, hiking, fishing, boating, and camping.

The University of Alabama's football team has won more than 740 games during its history.

Baseball legend Hank Aaron was born in Mobile in 1934. He was a professional baseball player for twenty-three seasons. At the end of his career he held records for runs batted in, total bases, and extra-base hits. Aaron still holds the record for the most home runs hit in one lifetime—755. He is also known for his quiet fight against discrimination in professional baseball. Hank felt that African Americans were not allowed to get administrative or coaching positions because of their race. In 1974, the National Association for the Advancement of Colored People gave Aaron the Spingarn Medal for his outstanding achievements in baseball.

Track and field star Jesse Owens was born in Oakville in 1913. He began to set world track and field records when he was still in high school. At the 1936 Olympic Games in Berlin, Owens won gold medals in the 100-meter dash, 200-meter dash, long jump, and 400-meter relay. At the time, German leader Adolf Hitler was claiming that all non-Europeans were inferior. With his four gold medals, Owens proved him wrong.

The Hank Aaron Award, which recognizes the best overall hitter in each league, was the first official award named after a player that was still alive.

QUICK FACTS

Hank Aaron was nicknamed "Hammerin' Hank."

Boxer Joe Louis was born in Lafayette in 1914. His twelve-year reign as heavyweight boxing champion is the longest ever.

There are three major league baseball **farm teams** in Alabama. The Birmingham Barons are the farm team for the Chicago White Sox; the Huntsville Stars are the farm team for the Oakland A's; and the Mobile BayBears are the farm team for the San Diego Padres.

The Jesse Owens Memorial Park, in Oakville, contains a 14-foot bronze statue of Owens running through the Olympic rings.

Brain Teasers

1

Which of the following athletes was not born in Alabama?

a. Carl Lewis

b. Ty Cobb

c. Joe Louis

d. Willie Mays

Answer: b. Baseball player Ty Cobb was from Georgia.

2

Which Alabama city is known as the Rocket Capital of the World?

a. Montgomery

b. Mobile

c. Huntsville

d. Birmingham

Answer: c. Huntsville is known as the Rocket Capital of the World.

3

What did Alabamian George Washington Carver invent?

Answer: Carver invented peanut butter. Alabama is third in the nation in the production of peanuts.

4

What new system of transportation was built in Montgomery in 1886?

Answer: The first electric trolley system in the world was built in Montgomery in 1886.

5

Which well-known basketball star played baseball for the Birmingham Barons?

Answer: Michael Jordan played baseball for the Birmingham Barons for one season in 1994.

6

Where does the name Alabama come from?

Answer: It is believed to come from two Choctaw words—*alba* (vegetable) and *amo* (gatherer).

7

Which body of water was the first in the New World to be accurately charted?

Answer: In 1519, Mobile Bay was successfully charted by Alonso Alvarez de Pineda.

8

In what year did Alabama's first school open?

Answer: Alabama's first school opened in 1799, near Mobile.

FOR MORE INFORMATION

Books

Aylesworth, Thomas G. *The South: Alabama, Florida, Mississippi.* Discovering America. New York: Chelsea House, 1996.

Bock, Judy and Rachel Kranz. *Scholastic Encyclopedia of the United States*. New York: Scholastic, 1997.

Gall, Timothy and Susan Gall, eds. *Junior Worldmark Encyclopedia of the States.* Michigan: U*X*L, 1996.

Hicks, Roger. *The Big Book of America*. Philadelphia: Courage Books, 1994.

Web sites

You can also go online and have a look at the following Web sites:

State of Alabama
http://www.state.al.us

Alabama Information Directory
http://www.alabamainfo.com

Alabama Archives Webpage for Kids
http://www.archives.state.al.us/kidspage/kids.html

Some Web sites stay current longer than others. To find other Alabama Web sites, enter search terms such as "Alabama," "Yellowhammer State," "Birmingham," or any other topic you want to research.

GLOSSARY

archeological: related to the study of early peoples through artifacts and remains

autobiographical: the story of a person's own life

bauxite: a clay-like rock, which is the main ore in aluminum

boll weevil: a small beetle that feeds on cotton bolls

boycott: to refuse to participate as a means of protest

broiler chickens: chickens raised for their meat rather than their eggs

desegregation: ending separations and restrictions based on race

fabricated metals: metals that are manufactured

farm teams: minor league sports teams that train players for major league teams

fossil fuels: fuels made from fossils, such as oil, coal, and natural gas

Freedom Riders: people who rode buses across the country to protest segregation

hydroelectricity: energy created by moving water

immunity: a resistance to certain diseases

irrigation: a system of pipes, ditches, or streams that supply fields with water

Mardi Gras: a festival whose name means "Fat Tuesday" in French, celebrated on the final Tuesday before Christian Lent

population density: the average number of people per unit of area

seaports: harbor towns or cities from which ships can drop off or pick up cargo

secede: to formally leave an organization or nation

segregation: forcing separation and restrictions based on race

spelunking: the recreational activity of exploring caves and caverns underground

stalagmite: a cone shaped stone formation that forms on the floors of caves

textile: fabric made by weaving or knitting

unconstitutional: not in agreement with the constitution of the United States

INDEX